FOOD SCIENCE

D0839616

SCIENCE 24/7

Animal Science

Car Science

Computer Science

Environmental Science

Fashion Science

Food Science

Health Science

Music Science

Photo Science

Sports Science

Travel Science

SCIENCE 24/7

FOOD SCIENCE

JANE P. GARDNER

SCIENCE CONSULTANT:
RUSS LEWIN
SCIENCE AND MATH EDUCATOR

Mason Crest

Mason Crest
450 Parkway Drive, Suite D
Broomall, PA 19008
www.masoncrest.com

Copyright © 2016 by Mason Crest, an imprint of National Highlights, Inc.

All rights reserved. No part of this publication may be reproduced or transmitted in any form or by any means, electronic or mechanical, including photocopying, recording, taping, or any information storage and retrieval system, without permission from the publisher.

Printed and bound in the United States of America.

Series ISBN: 978-1-4222-3404-4
Hardback ISBN: 978-1-4222-3410-5
EBook ISBN: 978-1-4222-8494-0

First printing
1 3 5 7 9 8 6 4 2

Produced by Shoreline Publishing Group LLC
Santa Barbara, California
www.shorelinepublishing.com
Cover Photograph: Dreamstime.com/Monkey Business Images

Library of Congress Cataloging-in-Publication Data

Gardner, Jane P., author.
        Food science / by Jane P. Gardner; science consultant, Russ Lewin, Science and Math Educator.
        pages cm. -- (Science 24/7)
        Includes bibliographical references and index.
ISBN 978-1-4222-3410-5 (hardback) -- ISBN 978-1-4222-3404-4 (series) -- ISBN 978-1-4222-8494-0 (ebook) 1. Food-
-Miscellanea--Juvenile literature. 2. Food--Research--Juvenile literature. I. Title.
TX355.G36 2016
664--dc23
                        2015004999

IMPORTANT NOTICE

The science experiments, activities, and information described in this publication are for educational use only. The publisher is not responsible for any direct, indirect, incidental or consequential damages as a result of the uses or misuses of the techniques and information within.

Contents

KEY ICONS TO LOOK FOR

Words to Understand: These words with their easy-to-understand definitions will increase the reader's understanding of the text, while building vocabulary skills.

Sidebars: This boxed material within the main text allows readers to build knowledge, gain insights, explore possibilities, and broaden their perspectives by weaving together additional information to provide realistic and holistic perspectives.

Series Glossary of Key Terms: This back-of-the-book glossary contains terminology used throughout this series. Words found here increase the reader's ability to read and comprehend higher-level books and articles in this field.

INTRODUCTION

Science. Ugh! Is this the class you have to sit through in order to get to the cafeteria for lunch? Or, yeah! This is my favorite class! Whether you look forward to science or dread it, you can't escape it. Science is all around us all the time.

What do you think of when you think about science? People in lab coats peering anxiously through microscopes while scribbling notes? Giant telescopes scanning the universe for signs of life? Submersibles trolling the dark, cold, and lonely world of the deepest ocean? Yes, these are all science and things that scientists do to learn more about our planet, outer space, and the human body. But we are all scientists. Even you.

Science is about asking questions. Why do I have to eat my vegetables? Why does the sun set in the west? Why do cats purr and dogs bark? Why am I warmer when I wear a black jacket than when I wear a white one? These are all great questions. And these questions can be the start of something big . . . the start of scientific discovery.

1. **Observe:** Ask questions. What do you see in the world around you that you don't understand? What do you wish you knew more about? Remember, there is always more than one solution to a problem. This is the starting point for scientists—and it can be the starting point for you, too!

Enrique took a slice of bread out of the package and discovered there was mold on it. "Again?" he complained. "This is the second time this all-natural bread I bought turned moldy before I could finish it. I wonder why."

2. **Research:** Find out what you can about the observation you have made. The more information you learn about your observation, the better you will understand which questions really need to be answered.

Enrique researched the term "all-natural" as it applied to his bread. He discovered that it meant that no preservatives were used. Some breads contain preservatives, which are used to "maintain freshness." Enrique wondered if it was the lack of preservatives that was allowing his bread to grow mold.

3. **Predict:** Consider what might happen if you were to design an experiment based on your research. What do you think you would find?

Enrique thought that maybe it was the lack of preservatives in his bread that was causing the mold. He predicted that bread containing preservatives would last longer than "all-natural" breads.

4. **Develop a Hypothesis:** A hypothesis is a possible answer or solution to a scientific problem. Sometimes, they are written as an "if-then" statement. For example, "If I get a good night's sleep, then I will do well on the test tomorrow." This is not a fact; there is no guarantee that the hypothesis is correct. But it is a statement that can be tested with an experiment. And then, if necessary, revised once the experiment has been done.

Enrique thinks that he knows what is going on. He figures that the preservatives in the bread are what keeps it from getting moldy. His working hypothesis is, "If bread contains preservatives, it will not grow mold." He is now ready to test his hypothesis.

5. **Design an Experiment:** An experiment is designed to test a hypothesis. It is important when designing an experiment to look at all the variables. Variables are the factors that will change in the experiment. Some variables will be independent—these won't change. Others are dependent and will change as the experiment progresses. A control is necessary, too. This is a constant throughout the experiment against which results can be compared.

Enrique plans his experiment. He chooses two slices of his bread, and two slices of the bread with preservatives. He uses a small kitchen scale to ensure that the slices are approximately the same weight. He places a slice of each on the windowsill where they will receive the same amount of sunlight. He places the other two slices in a dark cupboard. He checks on his bread every day for a week. He finds that his bread gets mold in both places while the bread with preservatives starts to grow a little mold in the sunshine but none in the cupboard.

6. **Revise the hypothesis:** Sometimes the result of your experiment will show that the original hypothesis is incorrect. That is okay! Science is all about taking risks, making mistakes, and learning from them. Rewriting a hypothesis after examining the data is what this is all about.

Enrique realized it may be more than the preservatives that prevents mold. Keeping the bread out of the sunlight and in a dark place will help preserve it, even without preservatives. He has decided to buy smaller quantities of bread now, and keep it in the cupboard.

This book has activities for you to try at the end of each chapter. They are meant to be fun, and teach you a little bit at the same time. Sometimes, you'll be asked to design your own experiment. Think back to Enrique's experience when you start designing your own. And remember—science is about being curious, being patient, and not being afraid of saying you made a mistake. There are always other experiments to be done!

1
A LOAF OF BREAD

"Can I get four raspberry croissants, please?" asked the customer. It was Jaxon's first day at his afterschool job at Cappa's Bakery. He was overwhelmed and stood by the cash register unsure what to do.

A girl about his age noticed his confusion and stepped in to help the customer. "Here you go, sir. That will be $7.50."

"Wow," said Jaxon, looking at the girl's name tag. "Thanks, Alina. It's my first day, obviously. I sort of froze there."

Alina laughed. "I get it. I've been working here for about three months. You get used to the pace. And there is so much to learn."

The crowd thinned out and Alina and Jaxon were called into the back of the store to help one of the bakers.

A tall man wearing an apron over his white clothing said, "Jaxon, Alina. I wanted to give you a tour of the kitchen. And to see if perhaps you'd be interested in learning about the art of baking." The apron that Mr. Cappa wore did little to stop the flour from covering his sleeves and pant legs.

"Yes, thanks," Jaxon said enthusiastically. "That's one of the reasons I was excited about taking on this job. I really wanted to learn more about baking and stuff."

"Well, then you came to the right place," said Mr. Cappa. He took a container of flour and several packets of ingredients from a shelf. "I was just getting ready to start the dough for tomorrow's special—we're featuring our famous cinnamon bread.

"I started this dough a few hours ago. It is already starting to rise."

"Rise? What do you mean by that?" Jaxon asked.

"This is why I decided to bring you back here—to teach you all about breads. At this point, the bread dough has just a few ingredients: milk, butter, eggs, sugar, and flour." He showed them the ingredients spread out on the counter.

"And this is what I think is the most important ingredient of all. Yeast." Mr. Cappa held up a jar of small, brown nuggets. "Yeast is what makes the bread rise."

"Yeast? What is it?"

"Actually," Mr. Cappa explained, "it's a fungus."

Alina wrinkled her nose. "A fungus? Really?"

"Yes, and it's alive right now."

Jaxon held his hand in front of him. "Ok, I am not sure if I'll ever eat bread again."

"Let me explain a bit." Mr. Cappa took a new loaf of bread off the shelf where it was cooling and cut it open. "See these holes in here? See how the inside of the bread is light and airy? This is because of the yeast."

While Jaxon and Alina chewed on a slice of the fresh bread, Mr. Cappa continued, "When yeast is added to flour and the other ingredients, it gets energy from a process called fermentation."

Through a mouth full of bread, Jaxon exclaimed, "Hey, I've heard of that!"

"Fermentation is how the yeast cells grow. They consume

Words to Understand

fermentation   the process of breaking down matter using yeast or bacteria

fungus   any plant part of this separate kingdom of living things; reproduces with the use of spores

yeast   a fungus used in the production of bread, beer, wine, and other products

the sugar we added to the dough as energy. As a result, the yeast releases a type of alcohol and carbon dioxide."

Alina stared at the bread in front of her. "Alcohol?"

"Don't worry, the alcohol burns off as the bread cooks in the oven! But it is the release of that carbon dioxide that makes the bread rise and makes these holes in the bread. The holes were bubbles of carbon dioxide that formed in the dough. In fact, if we put a little yeast in a cup with some sugar and water, it would turn all bubbly and foamy."

As they walked back to the counter at the front of the store, Jaxon admitted to Alina, "I had no idea that cooking and baking had so much to do with science."

Bad Yeast

Yeast is a fungus. And like all fungi, there are good species and bad species. The good species of yeast help make bread rise. The bad yeast can make you very sick. Candida albicans is a variety of yeast that can grow in the bloodstream and organs of people and animals. Like all yeast, this variety loves sugar and feeds on the sugar in our regular diets. The yeast takes up valuable nutrients such as iron from the body and leaves the blood very acidic. When left untreated, Candida albicans can destroy your digestive system, lower your immunity to disease, and cause things like headache, fatigue, dandruff, foggy thinking, and infections. Antibiotics may be prescribed to treat such an inflammation.

Try It Yourself

Yeast makes bread rise when it releases gas. You can see it in bread dough. Or, you could try this simple experiment to capture that gas from the yeast.

Materials:
- 1 packet of active dry yeast (check the date on the package to make sure it hasn't expired)
- 1 cup warm water
- 2 tablespoons sugar
- large balloon
- 1 liter plastic bottle, empty

1. Mix yeast and sugar with the warm water in the empty bottle. Stir until the yeast and sugar have dissolved.

2. What do you notice?

3. Place the balloon over the top of the bottle. Wait to see what happens.

4. What eventually happened?

5. Why do you think you were instructed to use warm water? Try the experiment again if you want, using cold water. What happens then?

6. What was the sugar for?

2
REDUCING
THE IMPACT

Alina went to talk with Mr. Cappa. "I just had a customer ask me why we continue to serve beef stew and roast beef sandwiches. She said that we are harming the environment. Is that true?"

Mr. Cappa gave the soup he was making on the stove one last stir and pulled a stool up to the counter. "Actually, Alina, there is a lot of evidence out there suggesting that eating beef can contribute to climate change. All meats actually, but beef seems to have an extreme impact."

"I don't get it," Alina admitted.

"Did you learn about global warming and greenhouse gases in school?" Mr. Cappa asked.

"Yeah, we did." Alina told him about what she had learned. "Global warming is a big part of climate change. It is the gradual increase in the temperature within Earth's atmosphere."

"But why is that happening?" Mr. Cappa asked. "Do you know about the greenhouse effect?"

Alina nodded. "Yes, the greenhouse effect can help explain why it gets hot inside a car on a warm sunny day. Sunlight enters the car and is absorbed by the seats and car mats and stuff inside. Some of that heat is reradiated back but the wavelength has changed. It is now infrared radiation, which has a longer wavelength. Not all of the heat can escape the car, so it is trapped and heats up the interior. And the same happens in our atmosphere. Sunlight, in the form of ultraviolet radiation, passes through the atmosphere. It is reradiated as infrared radiation and can't pass back out. It is trapped close to Earth's surface which warms it."

"You know your stuff. So what in the atmosphere keeps the heat trapped close to the surface?" Mr. Cappa inquired.

Alina was beginning to see where this was going. "Greenhouse gases. Things like carbon dioxide, water vapor, and methane are all greenhouse gases. Burning fossil fuels dumps a lot of carbon dioxide into the atmosphere. And . . ." Alina paused, "I'm guessing that cattle contribute a lot of, um, methane to the environment?"

"Exactly," Mr. Cappa said with a laugh. "As they eat, some of the waste from their digestion comes out in the form of a hot, stinky gas. But the impact of cattle goes beyond the obvious methane contributions. Herds of cattle require many more resources than other animals such as chickens or pigs. I read recently that beef cattle need 28 times more land and more than 10 times more water than chickens or pigs. This results in five times as much emission that can warm the atmosphere. As for the gases, it's

Words to Understand

carbon footprint the amount of carbon dioxide a person or a process produces during daily life

climate change the ongoing process in which the temperature of the Earth is growing over time

greenhouse gases heated air trapped beneath an atmosphere that no longer releases enough heat

infrared radiation a type of light invisible to human eyes, but which can create heat

fossil fuels energy-producing materials created by decayed animals and plants; these include oil and natural gas

methane a gas released during digestion by many animals

ultraviolet radiation another type of invisible light

wavelength the measurement of light that is the distance between individual waves within each type of light ray

not just the methane. Clearing the land will reduce the tree cover in an area, which reduces the amount of carbon dioxide taken from the atmosphere by those trees. That has an overall increase in the amount of carbon dioxide in the atmosphere."

"I bet those numbers are even more extreme when you compare it to vegetables," Alina said thoughtfully.

"Oh, most definitely. If you look at crops like white rice or potatoes and compare the calories people eat from those foods to beef calories, the beef needs more than 100 times more land to produce the same calories.

"Of course, some people say that without so many cows to feed, the supplies of corn and other grains that are fed to the cattle could be used to feed humans!"

Alina looked concerned. "So, if I choose to eat beef, am I doing something wrong?"

Mr. Cappa admitted the issue was a conflict for him as well. "It is a very complicated issue, Alina. There are so many sides to it, so much to take into consideration. It's political. It's emotional. But some experts say that to make a bigger impact on your carbon footprint, reduce the amount of beef you eat. That might be even more effective than not using your car."

"Wow," Alina sighed. "That's pretty significant. I guess reducing the amount of beef in our diets would go a long way, too, right?"

"Yes, and that's the approach I know many have started to take," Mr. Cappa agreed. "Many cultures in the world, including Japanese, Chinese, and Thai, use meat in their meals, but not as the main ingredient—almost more as an afterthought. Meals full of vegetables and rice, with small amounts of meat, seem to be environmentally friendly and healthy."

Alina shook her head. "I never thought about food as being so global before."

Carbon Footprint

Your carbon footprint can be defined as the total amount of greenhouse gases produced as a result of your daily activities. Usually it is expressed in terms of tons of carbon dioxide. Riding in a car, heating your home, flying in a plane, opting for plastic bags at the grocery store, buying plastic bottles of water, and eating hamburgers are all activities that increase your carbon footprint. There are many calculators and Web sites on the Internet that help track your personal or family carbon footprint and offer ways to reduce it. Check some of those out!

Try It Yourself

How did you get to school today? Did you walk? Ride your bike? Take the bus? Ride in a car? What impact does that have on your carbon footprint and the environment? Check out a carbon footprint calculator on the Internet. What small changes could you make in a day?

Materials:
- Internet access
- poster board
- pencils, markers

1. Find an Internet site that has a Carbon Footprint Calculator. There are many good sites out there. Check out these:

   www.epa.gov/climatechange/ghgemissions/ind-calculator.html

   footprint.wwf.org.uk

2. Pay attention to your daily habits. This can include your water usage while brushing your teeth, transportation to and from school and other activities, and shutting off unused electrical equipment. The calculator will probably have questions concerning all of these habits.

3. Answer the survey honestly.

4. What is your carbon footprint? What changes can you and the members of your household make to improve upon this?

5. Encourage your friends and family to try the questionnaire and reduce their footprint. Make a poster to share with others about ways to reduce your impact.

3
CARBOHYDRATES

Jaxon looked at the homemade jam that they used to fill the pastries sold at Cappa's. Then he tasted some and said, "You know, this jam isn't really all that sweet."

Alina took a small spoonful of the jam and tried it. "You're right. I bet we don't put much sugar in here at all."

"But fruit has natural sugar," said Jaxon. "Why would someone add sugar to it in the first place?"

"I think because most people like really sweet jam. I think sugar is a type of carbohydrate."

Jaxon disagreed. "No way, sugar isn't a carbohydrate. Things like bread and pasta are carbohydrates."

Alina took out her phone and got on the Internet. "Nope. Sorry, Jaxon. Sugars are simple carbohydrates. In fact, a very simple sugar, glucose, is the fuel for all your body's cells."

"Oh yeah," Jaxon said slowly. "Glucose, I forgot about glucose."

"Yep. And there are three kinds of carbohydrates: simple sugars, like glucose and fructose…"

Words to Understand

carbohydrate biological molecule containing oxygen, hydrogen, and carbon

glucose a simple sugar

"Which is found in fruits," Jaxon jumped in.

"Right. Another carbohydrate is sucrose. That's the sugar that we use in our foods and stuff. Sucrose comes from plants such as sugar cane, sugar beets, and…"

"Maple syrup!" Jaxon interrupted again. "Maple sugar is sucrose."

"The pure stuff is, that's right," Alina agreed, laughing at Jaxon's enthusiasm. "And the third major kind of carbs are complex carbohydrates. That's what you meant before when you said bread. Starch is an example. It's made of a bunch of sugar molecules together in a chain."

"So things like potatoes, pasta, and rice are all complex carbohydrates, right?"

Starchy foods such as potatoes
supply the body with complex carbohydrates.

"Yes. And so is fiber. Fiber is a complex carbohydrate. The thing with fiber is that your body doesn't break it down into the individual sugar molecules like it does with the starch. Fiber isn't a nutrient, really. But it is a necessary part of your diet that keeps the digestive system functioning well."

"So we need carbs, right?" asked Jaxon.

"Right," Alina answered. "But maybe not as many as most of us eat!"

Fiber

Fiber is a complex carbohydrate found in plants. Foods like corn, beans, whole grains, and apples all contain fiber. Most animals, humans included, don't break down fiber for use by their bodies. This is because fiber is actually cellulose found in the cells of plants. Cellulose helps protect the plant cells and provides the structure to the cells, which keeps a plant from falling over. This relatively tough carbohydrate can't be broken down in our bodies. Instead, fiber is necessary to keep the digestive system working properly.

Try It Yourself!

How many carbohydrates are you eating? What kinds are they? Simple sugars? Sucrose? Complex carbohydrates? Knowing what you are really eating is the first step to developing healthy habits.

Suggested Materials:
- notebook
- colored pencils or highlighters
- food labels
- cookbooks or cooking Web sites

1. For one day, log everything you eat. Every snack, every cracker, every apple. If possible, save any food wrappers that the food may have been packaged in.

2. Make a chart of your foods. List the calories, and the ingredients, and the nutritional information.

3. Are you overloading on the carbohydrates? What are you eating exactly? What changes can you make to your food choices to eat a more healthy diet?

4
GMO

"Alina, do you know what this means?" Jaxon held up a container of skim milk. "It says GMO free. What's that all about?"

Alina turned to answer. "I actually did a report on this for my science class just last month. GMO stands for 'genetically modified organism.'"

"What? Genetically modified organism? Sounds like something from a science fiction film."

"That's basically right." Alina agreed. "Sometimes a gene in an organism is altered on purpose by scientists. They may want to emphasize a specific trait. For example, using this method, it is possible to make plants that are immune to pesticides, or tomatoes with a longer shelf life, or papayas resistant to a deadly virus that was killing many of them. Scientists have been looking at ways to improve crop yields, increase resistance to pests and chemicals, and increase our food supply."

Jaxon thought a moment. "That doesn't sound like such a bad thing. If we can find ways to grow more food, then isn't that a good thing for everyone?"

"Well, there is actually a lot of debate in many countries swirling around the concept of GMOs," Alina explained. "Both sides of the issue—those who think it is a good idea and those who don't—have plenty of scientific data to back them up. It's complicated."

Words to Understand

gene molecular unit of heredity of living organisms

hormone molecules within the body that signal certain changes or responses

trait characteristics of an organism that are inherited from the passing of genetic material from parent to offspring

"Well, what are the concerns about GMOs?" Jaxon wondered.

"As far as I can tell, it is a health issue to the people who ultimately end up eating the foods. Opponents of GMOs show data that indicate that illnesses like allergies, digestive problems, and even reproductive disorders have increased since genetically modified foods have become a bigger part of our diet. There is concern about foods that have been genetically modified spreading their seeds or being introduced into the soil or water supply."

"Ok, I see. But what is the deal with this milk? Are the cows being modified genetically?" Jaxon held up the milk carton.

Some consumers are worried about the effect of GMO crops that enter the food chain directly or through animals that eat the crops.

"Actually, the genes of an animal don't need to be changed. But they can be fed food that has been, which will in turn affect their meat or milk," Alina explained. "Look here. That label indicates that the cows that produced the milk were not fed food that has been altered **genetically**. One of the biggest concerns with cows is that many of them are given a growth hormone called rBGH. The hormone was made from bacteria that were genetically modified. It is used to increase the milk production in a cow."

"So, does that milk taste different?"

"Officially, there is basically no difference. But some are concerned that cows given rBGH are more likely to get infections. They are then given more antibiotics to treat the infection and, in turn, the antibiotics end up in the milk you drink."

"But what about the other point of view?" Jaxon said. "Couldn't making plants better and stronger help?"

"Well, yes, that's the problem, of course," Alina said. "Assuming there are no long-term problems with GMOs, such plants could help feed many more people. Or they could be grown in places where they can't be grown now. The benefits to people could be large, but many people worry that the downsides would be too great. It's another example of science not having all the answers yet."

Genetically Modified Tomatoes

The first genetically modified food hit the supermarket shelves in the United States in 1994. This is when the Food and Drug Administration approved it for commercial use. The Flavr Savr tomato was genetically modified to slow the process of ripening and to keep the tomato from becoming soft. This would increase the shelf life of the tomato substantially. There was no indication of risks to human health or changes in the nutritional content. Production of this GM tomato stopped a few years later in 1997. Some say that it was the company's inexperience in growing and shipping tomatoes that lead to the failure of the product.

Try It Yourself!

Want to help others understand what is in their food? The best way is to show them. Show people the pros and cons of adding genetically modified foods to our diets. Let them make their own conclusions about what they want to eat.

Suggested Materials:
- Internet access
- poster board or construction paper
- markers, colored pencils

Go online! Research genetically modified foods and the effect they have on our diets and health. Create an informative pamphlet or poster to inform others. Include the following:
- Facts about genetically modified foods
- Information about which foods are typically modified and how
- Insight from farmers, consumers, and scientists
- Impacts on the food chain
- Impacts on humans

Photos, maps, and statistics can help give your pamphlet or poster more impact!

5
BROCCOLI?
NO THANK YOU

At the end of the afternoon, Jaxon was asked to remove the pastries that didn't sell and pack them in a bag. Cappa's donated the day-old pastries to a food pantry. Jaxon noticed that there were more of the broccoli and cheddar tarts left over than other types of tarts.

"Hmmm," he said to Alina, "I guess broccoli is not a big seller."

"I don't get that at all. I love broccoli. And those tarts are the best."

Jaxon disagreed. "Yuck. I am never very happy when broccoli shows up at the dinner table or in my salad. I don't think I am picky necessarily—I simply don't like broccoli. What is really wrong with that?"

Mr. Cappa overheard their conversation and came to discuss it with them. "What do you think the problem is with broccoli? Is it the texture? Or the smell? Do you like it raw rather than cooked?"

Words to Understand

chromosomes molecules within an organism which contain DNA
proteins large biological molecules consisting of amino acids

Jaxon didn't have to think about his answer. "I think broccoli is bitter. That's part of the reason I don't like it."

Mr. Cappa nodded. "There is a scientific reason for this. It all comes down to your genes."

Jaxon and Alina stared at him. "Really, your genes are to blame? Maybe Jaxon is really just a picky eater," Alina teased.

"I recently read a study that suggested otherwise," Mr. Cappa continued. "Your tongue is covered in taste buds. This is why you can taste sweet, sour, salty, and bitter. The taste buds are cells that have small taste receptors. The receptors combine with the food we eat, and then send a chemical to the brain which we interpret as taste."

Jaxon shook his head and said, "Sounds pretty complicated."

"It does, but really it isn't. The receptors on your tongue are made of proteins. And the proteins are made by your genes."

"And you get your genes from your parents," Alina broke in.

"Exactly," Mr. Cappa said. "So, I am guessing that Jaxon has a gene that interprets the taste of broccoli as bitter. And you, Alina, your genes don't do that. Your genes interpret the taste of broccoli differently."

Jaxon thought a moment. "So," he said slowly, "what you are saying is that the fact that I don't like broccoli is really my parents'

Say "ahhh"! Tiny bumps on your tongue send taste signals to your brain.

Umami

There is actually another taste your tongue can detect. This is the hard to define taste of umami. The word means "yummy" in Japanese. The taste is savory and rich. Foods like sun-dried tomatoes, soy sauce, miso, anchovies (right), shiitake mushrooms, and parmesan cheese all have umami qualities. When added to dishes, they add a certain deepness and richness to the taste. Umami is often difficult to identify, but when you taste it, you'll be pleased!

fault? They gave me my genes and my genes are interpreting the taste that way. Very interesting." He grinned.

Mr. Cappa held up his hands. "Now, don't go getting me in trouble here. But yes, you have 23 pairs of **chromosomes** on your DNA. You got one chromosome from your mother and one from your father. So it looks as if their contribution to your gene pool helped shape your taste in foods."

Jaxon rubbed his hands together. "I can't wait for dinner tonight. I hope my dad makes a big bowl of broccoli. We all need to have a little chat."

Try It Yourself

Your sense of smell and your sense of taste are closely related. Food tastes different when you have a cold and your nose is stuffy, doesn't it? Could you learn to tolerate your least favorite food if you couldn't taste it?

Materials:
- samples of foods; include several you don't like and several you do
- blindfold
- glass of water
- saltines
- partner
- notebook and pencil

1. Take a small bite of each food. Drink a sip of water and eat a saltine between each one to cleanse your pallet.

2. Make a note in your notebook of which foods you liked, and which you didn't.

3. Repeat the experiment again, only this time plug your nose.

4. What do you notice? Are your results the same? Be honest!

5. Consider repeating the entire experiment again. Only this time, crush or grind the foods up so you can't identify them by shape.

6. Have a partner blindfold you and give you small amounts of each food. The partner should note in the notebook your preferences with and without your nose plugged.

7. What did you find this time?

6
THE SCIENCE OF ICE CREAM

Jaxon had a new idea. Now that Cappa's Bakery was offering soup and sandwiches for lunch, perhaps they should try some homemade ice cream as well.

"Mr. Cappa," he turned to his boss, "I have an idea. Why don't we try to make some homemade ice cream? People do like to eat ice cream with their pie, right? We could offer that with our lunch menu."

Mr. Cappa scratched his head. "You know, Jaxon. You might be on to something there. But what do you know about making ice cream?"

Jaxon dug a thermos out of his backpack. "Actually, I made this at home last night."

Mr. Cappa grabbed a spoon. "Hmmm. Not bad. What does it involve?"

Jaxon was pleased to be teaching Mr. Cappa something. "I actually had to do several trials. I think I am getting closer now, though. I found out that it's more than just freezing milk or cream. There is chemistry involved."

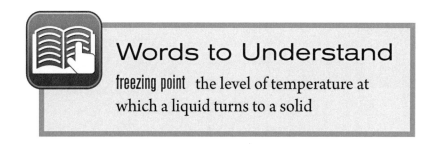

Words to Understand

freezing point the level of temperature at which a liquid turns to a solid

"And we all know chemistry is your favorite topic to discuss," Mr. Cappa said with a laugh. "Tell me about it."

"It all comes down to lowering the freezing point of the cream and milk. If that doesn't happen, then we'd end up with a mound of icy frozen milk with crystals in it, not a smooth creamy treat."

"What exactly do you mean by freezing point?"

"Substances have a temperature at which they freeze, or turn from a liquid to a solid, under normal conditions," Jaxon explained. "There are charts and tables that you can find on the Internet which give that information. For example, we all know that liquid water will freeze into ice at 32°F (0°C). But that temperature can be lowered if something else is added to the water.

"Remember that ice will absorb energy as it melts. Water in a solid form will turn into liquid water. If we use ice to cool down the milk, cream, and vanilla to make ice cream, the ice has to

The basic ingredients of ice cream: Just add ice and time.

Colligative Properties

Freezing points and boiling points are examples of colligative properties. A colligative property is a physical change that results from adding something to a substance. One example is adding salt to the ice to lower the freezing point. Car owners put a chemical called antifreeze to lower the freezing point of the liquids in the car engine. The point is, while water normally freezes at 32 degrees F (0 degrees C) and boils at 212 degrees F (100 degrees C) . . . that is not always the case! What is in the water or any other substance can greatly change those temperatures.

absorb energy from the ingredients themselves and the environment to cool down. Adding salt to the ice will lower the freezing point of the ice to below 32°F."

"But what does that mean?" asked Mr. Cappa. "I still don't understand why the milk freezes and why you need salt."

"If now the ice freezes at a lower temperature, then it needs to absorb even more energy from its surroundings and the ingredients. The ice is colder than it was before, and therefore the ice cream ingredients are colder than before and they freeze."

"Huh. Well, what do you know. You learn something new every day," Mr. Cappa said. "Let me make sure I've got this. To make ice cream you need milk, cream, sugar—plus other ingredients for different flavors—and ice. In order to make it so that the ingredients turn creamy and delicious you need to add salt to the ice so that the ice needs to absorb even more heat from the ingredients in order to melt. We make it more difficult for the ice to melt and get ice cream as a result."

Jaxon smiled. "That's it!"

"I like this idea, Jaxon. Good job. Order up the ingredients and we can start offering 'Jaxon's homemade ice cream' with our blueberry pies."

Try It Yourself

Ice cream is very easy to make on your own. In fact, you can make it in a plastic bag. All you need are the right ingredients, a lot of salt, and a friend.

Materials:
- 3 tablespoons of sugar
- 1 cup of whole milk or creamer
- ½ teaspoon vanilla or other flavored extract
- 1 quart-sized ziplock bag, heavy duty
- 1 gallon-sized ziplock bag, heavy duty
- ice
- rock salt
- other ingredients such as chocolate chips, crushed peppermint candies, or crumbled cookies

1. Put the sugar, milk, and extract into the quart-sized bag and seal tightly.

2. Put that bag inside the bigger bag. Add salt and ice in layers inside the bag and seal.

3. Toss the bag back and forth with your friend for about 10 minutes. Or simply kneed the bag.

4. Grab some spoons and enjoy!

7
FOOD ALLERGIES

Jaxon noticed a new sign over the counter at Cappa's. It read: "Before placing your order, please inform us if a person in your party has a food allergy."

"Hi Alina, what's this sign all about?" he asked.

"Afternoon, Jaxon. This is something the Board of Health is making all eating establishments put up. Food allergies are a big concern for many people these days, and it is important that everyone is aware of the issue."

"What exactly is an allergy? I have heard so much lately about people being allergic or intolerant or sensitive to food. My cousins don't drink milk without taking some sort of pill because it makes their stomach ache. What is the difference?"

Alina nodded. "I know. There is a lot of information out there. But my brother has an actual allergy to food. He is allergic to strawberries. His immune system misidentifies strawberries. The immune system is supposed to find and destroy germs like bacteria or viruses. His immune system identifies strawberries as a threat and then attacks it."

"I never heard of it that way," Jaxon admitted. "What happens if he eats strawberries?"

"Actually, an allergy to strawberries is pretty common. If he eats them, his throat gets tight and itches, his mouth and lips can swell, and he once got hives inside his mouth. Other people have it more severely and may develop an upset stomach, cramps, or a drop in blood pressure."

"Wow. What do you do for him if he accidentally comes in contact with one?"

Alina explained, "Well, first, he goes out of his way to avoid them. Sometimes even touching a strawberry to his skin will make him itchy and swell up. But my parents keep creams and lotions on hand that can help with the itch and the swelling. You would be surprised how many things use strawberry flavoring. Many ice creams and chocolates and desserts have strawberries. We have to really keep an eye on ingredients."

"Yeah, I know a kid from my baseball team who is allergic to peanuts. He has to watch everything he eats. It's hard to do things like eat in a restaurant for example, because you can't always be 100 percent sure what is in the food."

Words to Understand

establishment in this case, a noun meaning a place of business that is located in a building

immune system the body process that protects against outside agents such as germs, viruses, or bacteria

More than twice as many young people are allergic to nuts than they are to any other single food group.

"And it can be very dangerous if people with allergies come into contact with even a little bit of the food they are allergic to."

"But what about my cousins?" asked Jaxon. "They are lactose intolerant. That isn't the same, is it?"

Alina shook her head. "Not quite. From what I understand, that's a sensitivity to a food without being an actual allergy. The immune system is not involved in the same way. Lots of times the intolerance happens when the chemicals your body needs to digest the food aren't working right. Lactose is the sugar in milk and dairy products. People who have a lactose intolerance have trouble digesting the sugar."

"And they end up with upset stomachs and gas sometimes," Jaxon added.

"Exactly. There are many different levels of intolerance. People may suffer from all types of symptoms if they are sensitive to dairy or soy or gluten."

Jaxon turned and looked at the sign that was now hanging prominently over the counter. "Guess we really do need to have that sign."

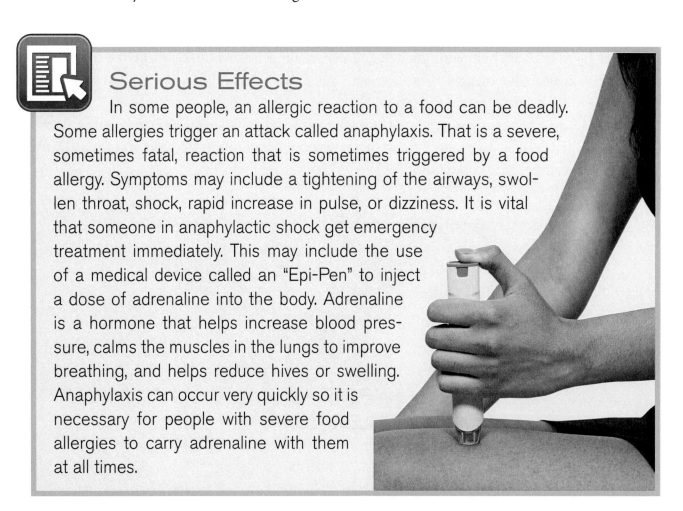

Serious Effects

In some people, an allergic reaction to a food can be deadly. Some allergies trigger an attack called anaphylaxis. That is a severe, sometimes fatal, reaction that is sometimes triggered by a food allergy. Symptoms may include a tightening of the airways, swollen throat, shock, rapid increase in pulse, or dizziness. It is vital that someone in anaphylactic shock get emergency treatment immediately. This may include the use of a medical device called an "Epi-Pen" to inject a dose of adrenaline into the body. Adrenaline is a hormone that helps increase blood pressure, calms the muscles in the lungs to improve breathing, and helps reduce hives or swelling. Anaphylaxis can occur very quickly so it is necessary for people with severe food allergies to carry adrenaline with them at all times.

Try It Yourself

People with food allergies must be very diligent about checking ingredients on food labels. Some processed foods can contain small amounts of foods that can cause severe allergic reactions. Do you know what to look for on a food label to keep yourself, your family, and your friends safe?

Materials:
- notebook and pen
- access to a supermarket or multiple food labels
- Internet access

1. Pick a food allergy you'd like to investigate. Common food allergies include eggs, dairy, soy, peanuts, wheat, and sesame.

2. Use Internet resources to identify the terms and names of substances that are related to your allergen. For example, durum, semolina, and spelt are all types of wheat. These ingredients in a food could cause an allergic reaction to someone with a wheat allergy.

3. Make a list of 15–20 foods that you and your friends enjoy eating. Include all different types of food including cereals, frozen treats, prepackaged foods, and other things.

4. Find packaging for each of the food items. Examine the ingredients of each one. Would someone with the allergy you are looking at be able to eat it?

5. Make a list of the acceptable and unacceptable foods. What did you find?

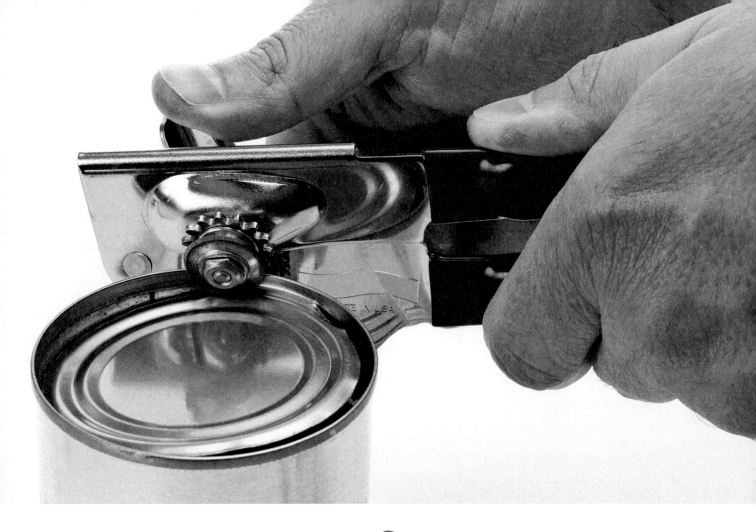

8
WHAT'S IN A CAN?

"Oh! Don't use that can." Alina made a grab for the can Jaxon had in his hand.

"Whoa. What are you talking about?" She had startled him.

Alina pushed the can of tomatoes back from the edge of the counter. "It's bulging. See that?"

Jaxon took a closer look. "Yeah, it is. So what? What does that mean? I thought maybe the can was just too full."

Alina shook her head. "No, it could be dangerous to eat. Haven't you heard of botulism?"

"Botulism? No, what's that?"

"Botulism is food poisoning caused by bacteria," Alina explained. "Clostridium botulinum is the group of bacteria that causes it. It can be found in soil or in some water sources, but it has the ability to survive in some extreme conditions. The bacterium can survive in cans or preserved foods and even a little bit can make a person very, very sick."

Jaxon stared at the bulging can of tomatoes with distrust. "You mean, this can could have made a lot of people sick?"

Alina nodded. "Food like vegetables, pork and ham, honey, and corn syrup are the most common ones that may carry the botulism bacteria."

"How would you know if it was a bad batch? Does it smell funny?"

"Not necessarily," she said. "Typically the person becomes sick to their stomach and may vomit. There is usually diarrhea involved, too. But some very severe symptoms may occur which would mean the person would have to be hospitalized."

Jaxon didn't touch the can but looked over it to see if he could read the expiration date. "But right here, it says it won't expire for another six months."

Alina blew her bangs up off her face. "Were you listening? The can is bulging because of a bacterium that is inside. It isn't because it is expired. The tomatoes weren't completely clean. Or maybe the metal used to make the can had the bacterium. But it isn't because of the expiration date."

Alina put the can under the counter. "In fact, expiration dates are hard to figure out."

"What do you mean? Isn't an expiration date the date after which the food goes bad?" Jaxon had figured that was the case.

Alina shrugged her shoulders. "Well, think about it. If you take a container of cottage cheese and put it in a refrigerator at a lower temperature than another fridge, then it will stay colder longer. But if you keep it on the counter, then the expiration date isn't correct, right? It would go bad long before then."

"That's right," Jaxon agreed. "And sometimes meats and things look kind of discolored in the packaging. You aren't really sure what happened to it before you bought it at the store, I guess."

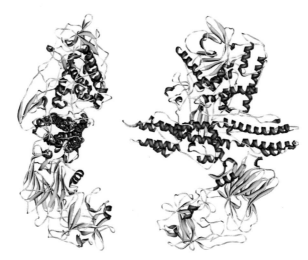

This colored micrograph shows the bacteria that causes botulism.

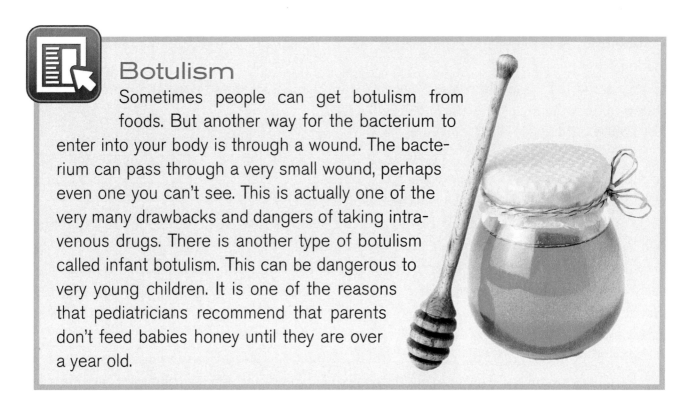

Botulism

Sometimes people can get botulism from foods. But another way for the bacterium to enter into your body is through a wound. The bacterium can pass through a very small wound, perhaps even one you can't see. This is actually one of the very many drawbacks and dangers of taking intravenous drugs. There is another type of botulism called infant botulism. This can be dangerous to very young children. It is one of the reasons that pediatricians recommend that parents don't feed babies honey until they are over a year old.

"My mom goes by the sniff test, although that's not really scientific."

"Is that what I think it is? She sniffs it to see if it smells bad?"

Alina nodded. "Yeah. And we've never gotten sick from eating her food."

"Okay," Jaxon agreed. "But it still sort of makes me nervous. Things are a lot more complicated than I used to think they were."

Try It Yourself

How long would a carton of milk really last in the refrigerator? Design an experiment to try and find out. You don't have to drink the milk if it spoils– perhaps just smelling it would be a good idea.

Suggested Materials:

- paper
- pencil

1. Devise your hypothesis.

2. What is your procedure? List the steps.

3. How many trials will you do? What is your controlled variable? Your independent variable?

4. Predict what your results will be.

5. Explain what you think you would see.

6. Draw a conclusion.

Note: If possible, try this out! Be sure to keep track of the purchase date and the sell by date. Watch the temperature within the refrigerator and use your nose to judge if it is spoiled or not. Have fun!

9
CONCLUSION

Food Science. As Jaxon remarked several times, so much about food and cooking and nutrition has to do with science. Science touches everything from how the food is grown and how it impacts the environment, to how we know if it is spoiled or not.

Food is a huge part of our lives. It helps give us energy to go about our daily lives, provides the nutrients and minerals to grow, develop, and learn in school, and food is also a centerpiece for our social wellbeing. Families and friends bond and communicate over food. It is what we are all about.

But so many people in the world do not have enough food. Between 2010 and 2012, the United Nations estimated that one out of every eight people in the world was undernourished. They do not receive enough food and nutrients to keep them healthy. That figure is staggering. The problem is not just in third-world countries, though, of course, they are by far the hardest hit. In poor countries, a lack of money for farming, for seed, for water makes food shortages worse. When people do not have enough energy to work, the problem compounds and they are not able to grow their own food. Add to that the problems of weather and climate change that have made, temporarily or permanently, once-fertile areas into regions of drought and famine. Closer to home, poverty in the United States has created a growing food crisis. In some counties, more than 30 percent of the young people are considered undernourished. Food banks are reporting larger numbers than ever of people coming to obtain nutrition basics. Many studies have shown that the world and its people have the capacity to feed everyone. The problem is that the food is not distributed evenly across the globe.

Science will play a part in this ongoing problem, too. Scientists of the future will need to focus on producing more food to feed a growing population. This will involve everything from improving soil quality, preventing runoff, and reducing water pollution to developing new crops that may produce higher yields. There is a lot of work to be done. Will you play a role?

It is not necessarily the first thing you will think about when you think about food, but soil and the quality of soil is very important when it comes to growing crops. Want to see for your-

For millions of people around the world, deliveries of donated food like this one can mean the difference between life and death.

Be part of the solution: Find ways to help feed others, such as working at a shelter, soup kitchen, or food bank.

self what that would look like? At home, plant three bean plants in three small containers. Keep all the variables the same: ensure the plants get the same amount of sunlight and water, use the same type of plant seeds, and the same type of soil. However, use the correct amount of fertilizer in one container, add twice the amount in a second one, and add none to the third. What do you think will happen? Give the plants a few weeks, and look at the result. What do you find? What does this tell you about the need to have good quality soil to grow plants?

The way we think about our food is beginning to change. As global citizens we all need to realize that what we eat could have a wide reaching impact on the environment as a whole. Try to educate yourself on the options you have and make informed decisions. It might just make a difference.

Food Science 24–7: Concept Review

Chapter 1

The next time you bite into a sandwich think about the fact that a living microorganism played a very important role in making the bread you are eating.

Chapter 2

The food choices you make can have an impact not only on your health, but on the environment as a whole. As Alina discovered, some choices are more ecologically friendly.

Chapter 3

Not all carbohydrates are created equal, and not all carbohydrates react the same in your body. As Jaxon found out, there are many carbohydrates in our everyday diets.

Chapter 4

Would you eat foods that were modified to enhance certain characteristics such as flavor or resistance to spoilage? You may already be doing that.

Chapter 5

Are you a picky eater? This chapter explains how it might not be your fault—it might be a matter of genes!

Chapter 6

Jaxon explained how the ice cream-making process is more than a way to get a tasty treat—it is actually an experiment in chemistry.

Chapter 7

Food allergies are a very serious condition. Jaxon and Alina find out just how important it is to be aware of them.

Chapter 8

Not all food is safe. This chapter looked at the problems that can arise if food becomes spoiled.

FIND OUT MORE

Books

Does your school have a garden? Would you like to help start one? Encourage your parents and teachers to take a look at this book with you. Who knows what will happen!
Bucklin-Sporer, Arden and Rachel Pringle. *How to Grow a School Garden: A Complete Guide for Parents and Teachers.* Portland, Or.: Timber Press, 2010.

Do you like food? And cooking? And learning about science? Then this book is for you!
Heinecke, Liz Lee. *Kitchen Science Lab for Kids: 52 Family Friendly Experiments from Around the House.* Minneapolis: Quarry Books, 2014.

Does the idea of getting some of the protein in your diet from worms and bugs sound interesting? Do you like being grossed out? Then check out this book. Food science can be pretty icky too!
Solheim, James and Eric Brace. *It's Disgusting and We Ate It! True Food Facts From Around the World and Throughout History.* New York: Aladdin, 2001.

Web Sites

Want to know more about avoiding genetically modified foods in your diet? Refer to this Web site for some helpful hints.
www.nongmoproject.org/learn-more/

Do you, or someone you know, have food allergies? Check out this Web site. There are many recipes, designed for people who have all sorts of food allergies or intolerances.
community.kidswithfoodallergies.org/clip/cupcakes-with-a-whipped-ganache-frosting-egg-milk-peanut-andamp-treenut-free

Want to look at what your carbon footprint is like? Here is one Web-based quiz you can take.
www.nature.org/greenliving/carboncalculator/

Series Glossary of Key Terms

alleles different forms of a gene; offspring inherit one allele from each parent

chromosomes molecules within an organism which contain DNA

climate change the ongoing process in which the temperature of the Earth is growing over time

force in science, strength or energy that comes as a result of a physical movement or action

frequency number of waves that pass a given point in a certain period of time

friction the resistance encountered when an object rubs against another object or on a surface

gene molecular unit of heredity of living organisms

gravity the force that pulls objects toward the ground

greenhouse gases gases in the atmosphere that trap radiation from the sun

inertia tendency of an object to resist change in motion

laser an intensified beam of light

lift the force that acts to raise a wing or an airfoil

momentum the amount of motion by a moving object

semiconductor a substance that has a conductivity between that of an insulator and that of most metals

sustainable able to be maintained at a certain rate or level

traits characteristics of an organism that are passed to the next generation

wavelength a measurement of light that is the distance from the top of one wave to the next

Picture Credits

Dreamstime.com:
Ljupco 8
Miflippo 10
Carrieanne 12
Ukrphoto 16
Gmargittai 17
Shaiith 18
Endostock 20
Mateno 22
Piksel 24
Savageultralight 25
Akihoko74 26
Ajafoto 28
GourmetPhotography 29
Darac 32
Dsollphoto 33
Robeo 34
Whitestar 1955 36
Mneucla 38
Dolgachov 40
Monkey Business Images 42

Newscom: Rosalee Yagihara 21, Ismael Mohammed/UPI 41
Ayacop/Wikimedia: 37

About the Author

Jane P. Gardner has written more than a dozen books for young and young-adult readers on science and other nonfiction topics. She became an author after a career as a science educator. She lives in Massachusetts with her husband, two sons, plus a cat and a gecko!

About the Consultant

Russ Lewin has taught physics, robotics, astronomy, and math at Santa Barbara Middle School in California for more than 25 years. His creative and popular classes and curriculum include a hands-on approach to learning and exploring that instills a love of science in his students.

Index